Scattered Blood Drops

Περσεφόνη Ανέμη

BookLeaf Publishing

India | USA | UK

Presentation by *BookLeaf Publishing*

Web: www.bookleafpub.com

E-mail: info@bookleafpub.com

ISBN: 9789358737653

First edition 2023

To those that are my true family.

To all those that escape the same nightmares night after night...

And... Tay, Maya, Jazz, Daphnee, Emily, thank you for walking in the darkness with me.

ACKNOWLEDGEMENT

My mother has always been my greatest supporter and fan, and this is one of the ways I can say thank you for the breath she gifted me – and the eternal love for books and poetry.

To her, my soul sister Helena and my lovely husband Nick that are always calming forces in my life, as well as the few selected friends I made over the years, my love and gratitude.

PREFACE

Taking the road less travelled by may end up in
Alice's maze...
Watch out for the black rabbit... It bites!

My long lost Blue

Your scalpel mumbles eagerly in your hands
thin
shinning
brand new as it reflects the street lamps.
If you make a cut in Blue
you discover it hides bows inside.
Dolphin-shaped arrows
tear apart everything that,
soft and resigned,
chooses to sink in darkness.
Abyss is only defined by Abyss
and that is her end.

The blade falls
heavy
Crunching sounds follow its path
the blood is not enough for all
We hunger!
Spoonful by spoonful
the sea was eaten up.
Fire takes over
it dissolves into droplets upon naked skin
her carvings on flesh resemble
a new-born language.

Birds do not die singing
they sell their wings
for dreams they never see.
Feather after feather
for a futile dive in lead.
They exchange their last bunch
for a second chance.
In the end, they die of cold…

Welcome to my Nightmare

Here
on the edge of a cliff
over a roaring sea
I remember…

Grey
children's laughter
a wooden rocking horse in the corner fades out
like in the old silent movies.
Does not move.
Nothing moves.
A kid with a lifeless smile
frozen.
The eyes scream of panic.
A child with a knife.
A mouth lies cut on the floor, melting
blue drops on the walls.
The child scratches its head
discarding it piece by piece on the ground.
The floor is fake
it's a white table really.
The child is almost naked
people are gathered around it.
The table is set for dinner.
They are laughing

everyone is laughing.
Disfigured mouths around the child
circling the table
hungrily snatching flesh pieces out off the air
with their forked tongues.
Laughing
Laughing.
Their jaws spread open to feed on the future.
Sawed teeth etch their fairytales
tear their dreams to pieces
gut their toys
devour their locks of hair
that soil the white tablecloth.
Laughing laughing laughing…

Here
in a field packed with daisies
stamped on after the Sunday picnic
I remember…

A full-body mirror.
Behind it lies a granite face
hard
chiseled on stone
striking
a teenage girl.
Her clothes a colorful embrace on the floor
forming a pigeon's nest
around her thin ankles

laugh-less clothes
grim
mournful.
Winter targets and pierces through sparrows
outside her window.
Nothing survives during this season
nothing that chooses to be alone.
The teenage girl is in the process of titivation.
She is plucking her eye-brows out
tears her eyes
carves her forehead
bruises her chest
pulls her nails out.
Delicate scars decorate her naked wrists.
Her legs spread open.
Her two naked legs could weave a whole story
as they whip the air.
She lies on top a satin bed.
«Oh, look how beautiful satin is!» everyone
exclaims.
She is terrified
shaking
Her legs continue to open.
Satin is slippery
like the day she almost drowned in a
moss-covered swamp.
Satin reminds her of the swamp
despite it being white.
A spotlight shines on her.

Her clavicles break under pressure.
Her hands tied with animal entrails.
She screams
thrashes about
is violated
again and again
Satin is dyed purple like the first days of
Spring…

Here
on the eve of the century
moments before Eastern perfume chokes the
resurrection
I remember…

Everyone running in a circle.
Thirty children.
Thirty children dance in that circle
as if celebrating their victory.
They have a woman in the middle.
She is wearing a dress
full of sunflowers and pine needles.
You can't see any of that, though.
The dress is white.
The woman is the children's mother.
They spin around her singing
holding matches.
They have poured gasoline on her.

They want their mom to not smell of death
anymore.
She is holding a scalpel.
Everyone running in a circle.
She tears her flesh
cuts fibers
pieces
pulls out anything that flails about
takes her warm, pulsing womb out.
Cuts it into thirty pieces.
A river of dead children pours out.
Mouthful by mouthful
she feeds her womb to her children.
She drives the scalpel deeper still
again and again.
She screams for her mother.
Her tears are pink
they mesh with the black of her belly.
She roots out life from within her.
Holding her heart in her hands
her soul in her mouth
everyone running in a circle.
And she spits it…

A child

An itch
irritating
on my hands
my palms
between my fingers
it burns
madness burns upon my hands!
I scratch
uproot the skin
it tears
black and white strands commit suicide towards
the floor
like a 30s movie
thank the Gods
I exist…
I still bleed…!

A saw
in the edges of our gaze
between two silent breaths
hides a saw
grinding
scratching
testing its claws
tasting

licking its lips
suddenly
IT BITES!

The ground trembles
terror-infused screams are heard from the sea
caves
steam breaks the watery surface
cracking it
being unleashed
making everything white – like bleach.
Swan wings
fights of birds to the death
drowning yelps from beaks…

A child
A child within a child within a child…
A child is yelling
GET IT OUT!
Flay its way!
Chisel!
Uproot!
Detach!
Dismember!
Birth it to now!
NOW!
GET IT OUT!

Treasure island

Grey rocks
full moon
sea waves, salty like death
barren land
infertile.
Land on the verge of hunger
on the banks of typhoon.
Five-limbed creatures
butchered
crawl amidst the edges of existence
extracting breath from the moonlight
eyes filled with razor blades
brass nails
unevenly-cut titanium teeth
swords protrude from their backs
made of dust and poison.

Madness upon their hair roots
drips on the temples faster than blood
stings more than guilt.
Their skin glows cyan
like an old fossil.
Their eyes wide open
as if they know nothing but surprise
fear

lidless eyes.

Their offspring resurrected
red
skinned
find refuge in the niches of the granite
children made of skin and shadow
with an ashen stench upon their transparent
clothes
and chains that rattle between their bones
incinerated children.

Their women dressed in black
skinless chests
open legs
birthing tomorrow with every breath
never stopping
screaming!
They make way into their guts with their own
hands
digging
seeking oblivion with frenzy
being forgotten
grinding their teeth
jaws that sharpen time
that break sobs into a thousand pieces.

They move from cliff to cliff gliding
almost forcefully caressing the stone

dressed in shreds of previous lives
rotten memory pieces
a moment before – just a moment
madness
overthrowing heavy wooden tables
tearing whole houses up
uprooting trees
sinks her nails above the hips
and claims – without any conditions
that
which was already hers…

The Harlequin

Many the hopes to start anew
yet courage faints
too light to bend the unshaken conviction of
stone.
Shadows on the walls
gazing with their non-existent yet ablaze eyes
demanding
with their painfully soundless cries
with their fleshless steel hands
their nails created of guilt
their faces made of tears
engraved on granite like third degree iron burns.

With the silent persistence of those that know to
wait
those that grasp the knowledge
of why the void seems to expand
as soon as the Abyss summons.
Once the gates open
and nightmare-inducing creatures spill out
all the old, innocent, childish toys of yours
disfigured
terror-birthing
night-cloaked.

Bloody teddy bears with maggot infested seams
skeleton dolls dressed with daggers
copper horses with broken glass for teeth
razor-sharp pages in books.
And that obscenely colourful
unnaturally massive
harlequin made of trembling extremities
with the lidless, glass eyes
the torn into a permanent gangrenous smile
the open facial wounds
the yellow, bile teeth…
Calmly waiting for your show to end
so that he can creep the audience out
with his unique
crystalized
deadly
perforated pink laugh…

Rebirth

Mould … darkness …
A scent like an animal's sweat.
A door squeaks as it slowly closes
like bones that cannot lift any more weight.
I open my eyes… close them again…
There's cold metal under my naked body
a sheet covers my ruptured sleep.
I wake up in the morgue.
A name tag on my toe declares who I was.
The sheet, white, covers what I left behind.
An engraved sign upon untouched flesh
my insides
prophesizes what I will become…

Ashes fall indolently from the ceiling.
Burnt feathers
I smell mint… hyoscyamus… and lit lavender.
Children's faces
around… inside… on me, like protection spells
children's faces dingle with happy sounds in the
air as I rise.
I learn to balance
I learn the first step, then the next.
I learn breath and immediately suck it like water.
I learn to cry

and I let my face make rain.
I learn to laugh
and wild, moonless cries escape my sawn lips.

I choose skin to dress… sword… anger!
I cut one breast off to better balance War.
I tightly fasten my leather boots, showing metal
up to the point it scrapes my bones.
I carve my hands: a name, a town, a dream…
I imprint those on my hands
shredding the skin and reuniting sounds with
blood.
Once I may be called a witch, yet I never feared
fire…

Everything now rests upon my hands
and they shall follow me from there until I make
them justice.
Until
ripping me to pieces
they fly from my hands bleeding
dripping amniotic fluid
they stand before me shaking
and looking me in the eyes.

Resignation

Another day...
Another long marathon
down the mill of human destruction.
Another bruised pause between breaths
to toughen the muscles
and swallow the scream of tearing flesh.
Another disintegrating moment of pure laughing
madness...
Another stretched hour down the rabbit hole
with no exit...
Another darkness to choke and chain...
Another demon to outrun and befriend...
Another crime to leave unsolved
and unreported...
Another marvellous self-destructive dance upon
sharpened glass...
Another dress made of poison ivy...
Another day in paradise
for an outcast fallen angel...
Another wingless walk on clouds that drift off...

I resign...

Just for tonight
I fill in the form

and resign my human flesh...
Just for tonight
I shall embrace my liquid pain...
I shall become the sky's bitter tear
falling in an eternally frozen Icarian leap of
faith...
I shall fall on your lips...
I shall take your scent with me
as I run down your skin and onto the ground...
I shall carry you with me
renamed and re-owned...
Clean and forgiven
I shall claim you...
Just for tonight...
Just this once...
And kiss you as you have never been kissed by a
sinner before...

Hungry pigeon

Eyes of a predator
nails of a hurricane
walking like a snake across stone
shadows born out of iron.
The curse is at its zenith.
The Pharaoh is now awakened
he slowly spreads his arms
and mummified grasshoppers jump on the
sleepwalking conscience.
The firstborns are dead on some palace's steps
I am the only one that survived, mother...

In a basket
in a cage made of reeds they wrapped my baby
dreams.
In a river of blood
in black waters my miniscule white survived,
secretly floating
undisclosed
disguised...

Engraved paths across the forehead
on the back
ditches made of whips
scars from chains on the wrists

crumbling bones
flesh made of hessian
fragments of cheesecloth for hair
and a mouth sawed shut by wrath's thread
made of silenced and raped screams.
Two coins in place of the eyes
the rust on them smells more potently than a
corpse.
The scent is carved upon memory
as the prophecy is chiselled on the rock with
nails.

The whole body a lament
a bitterness
a puzzle hidden for centuries
a secret of shame.

I can't bear it anymore, mother!
I am belching flesh spheres and give birth to
more.
Somewhere inside, something rots...
From time to time
it opens two eyes
like a pigeon
and gazes at me
coldly
calculatedly
on its one side

as if I were the globe that rolled down the wrong
downhill
and I confuse it!
Where is it supposed to take the fucking olive?
Where?

I have no answer to offer
so it nibs
eats
grows stronger.
And that eye
the one eye
made of glass
black
like the waters from my first live memory...
I swim away from it ever since
but it ends up inside me every time.
And my white is not enough
simply cannot
wave its hand and send it away...

Reconstruction

A body
naked
red
fleshless.
A body inside a cocoon.
Does not wait for its transformation into a
butterfly
awaits for oxygen to be depleted.
Hides a surprise
with crunching sounds.
A terror
unspoken
deep
shadowy and crawling.
It shall reveal itself by bombing foundations
it shall be birthed by massacring intestines
it shall take its first breath by turning bones into
dust.
This is how it must be done!

This is how it was always done
When revolution took flesh.
With scythes
pickaxes
cement blocks

it would flood the streets in blood.
Butchering old
ancient
inherent rotten regimes.

Like a baby, that, in order to come out
needs to split the mother in two
and slice her in four
six
a thousand
for the rest of its life
All new that is founded
needs building materials…

Human

I took hold of my quill and wrote the word
"Human"
and froze…
A heavy word…
Like a hand grabbing my trachea
and squeezing it…
Human…
Black dots on a sea of white
like guilt…
No, let me write something beautiful…
Human…

An image flashes in my mind
like a blasting gun barrel!
The scenery cleans up from the smoke…
A smile of sweaty madness
sharp shards shoved inside wide-open jaws
forever transfixed in a soundless scream of
agony
shining from the blood
of all the animals they devoured.
Glassy painted eyes
eyelids nailed on the hollow skull
with steel nails
empty

blurred mirrors of a cracked tomorrow
that takes too long to arrive
still
like a nightmare
that lurks at nightfall…

Sounds flood the sail cloth…
Terror-birthing sounds
of other-worldly creatures
that annihilate the very last bloody drop
the breath
that escapes from the lips towards the
slaughtered light.

Human…
Who knows the moment is upon us…
That human is no longer grouped
or unique.
That was not…
Is not…
Is never going to be human again…
And now knows it well…

Night walk

It's dark again...
Another walk down the alleyways of despair
like a ritual
a punishment seemingly never ending.
Tears smear the city walls
they slowly slip down concrete
like blood from a fresh wound
they leave their imprints on breaths
without asking for consent.

She stands alone
a black and white figure.
Her life a book
forgotten
on some shelf in a torn down shop.
Eyes blasé
lips red
hollow clack clack from her heels
that time has tried his jaws on.
Clothes on her
like a lover's hands she no longer desires.

Crawling shadows everywhere
lurking
stalking.

Their nails imperceptibly scratch the stones
eager
almost tasting her fear
her screams of pain
the white moment of panic.

Her flesh shines translucent in the moonlight
like sin sliced with a knife
alabaster that escaped Hades' wells.
She stops under a blinking streetlamp
a soft wind carries garbage from the asphalt
they caress her naked ankles.
She takes a deep breath.
The city enters her
softly
sounding like silk.
She awaits for them
maybe tonight they manage the final hit...

Echoes

I am looking at her in terror
she sits across from me in darkness
her elbows on her knees
her head in her hands
she has clasped her palms on her forehead.

She talks
for centuries she carries on a uniquely annoying
lament
the torturing sound of her grating voice
reaches me crawling
dripping bile
unrecognisable to my ears.
She speaks of pain
wounds
complaints…
Sudden silence…

She lifts her gaze off the floor and looks at me
with white eyes
hollow
filled with glue
and lava.
She thrusts her nails in her forehead
deep

deeper.
Her blood streams down her face in rivulets
like punishment
like lines death row inmates mark on a wall to
end their suffering…

Her hands start creating distance from one
another
they tear
they plough the forehead skin.
Her mouth opens like a chasm
as if she wants to taste her own blood
like a redemptive poison.
Yet she does not drink.
She continues this endless movement
until her jaws are no longer bounded by flesh.
Her teeth reflect the minimal light
poems shoved into the gums
without pattern
her lips filled with broken stitches
needle marks
repeated traumas
filled with holes…

And she screams!
She screams
and the walls tremble
the cups on the shelves shatter

small glassy drops rain upon us
stinging.

She screams for the second time
and the house shakes
is threatened
the masonry shrinks
is afraid of her.
She removes her hands from her forehead
strands of hair scatter on the floor
like ashes after a fiery explosion
skin pieces escape her fingers
like embryos kicked out of Heaven
committing suicide towards the only place that
will accept them
downwards…

She screams for the third time
with her hands spread to her sides
standing
barely dressed
flayed.
She pulls one scream after another from her
lungs
her palms open
huge nail wounds upon them
like a Christ deprived of miracle
blinded

with boiling intestines
with steam rising from her every pore
with lit charcoal in her chest
fumes out her mouth.

She screams as if she is unable to stop.
She throws her head back and screams
in a way only she can.
My eardrums explode
the world becomes pain
a red pulsing light.

More are to come
now I know.
Each will come
and hammer a chosen sense
to the point of annihilation
until only pain remains
signalling to my automated corpse
that it still functions...

Insect phobia

An insect
inside my mind
within my thoughts
an insect has made its lair.
Black
huge
its eyes locked on mine
It fills the screen
the crowd runs panicked to the flashing exits
scattered pop-corn on the floor
like brains that, in love,
followed the bullet that pierced them into a new
adventure.
The insect stalks
to reap the dawn of my breath
it waits…

A loud buzz reaches my ears
that intense sound that resembles vertigo
it flashes on and off
brings images upon its wake
carries them
like small trash in the wind.
Human-like insects.
Women with antennas on their heads

naked
flayed
shaking.
With wide belts on their waists
that their children hang from
nymphs.
With huge crystal wings
dripping bitterness.
With long strands of unkempt hair
that they tie into knots
to remember all that was forgotten.

Women that were fooled.
They thought dreamy
colourful and light wings they were winning.
Women with hate grazing their gaze
it spreads
like an icy wind in sealed off ball rooms
you can hear it
above the buzzing of their collective breaths.
Their shadows taint the red backdrop of my
flesh.

They are getting closer!
But they cannot reach me
they cannot jump over the ruins
yet they shall stand there.
Thus they shall always stand
hundreds of women

hating
their hands grasp the nothingness above the
chasm
forever reaching
painfully relentless.
Their eyes birth that metallic startle of fear
when someone touches your back
as soon as you walk in and lock behind you.
And their horrific buzzing!
I want to rid me of that sound!
Alas
I fear
that after it
more terror-birthing sounds come
crawling
bone-breaking
flesh-detaching they shall arrive
to feed on whatever is left…

Solitude

The earth's foundations are ablaze…
Mother is burning!
Simoom invades through the cracks on the wall.
Ashes fall in his stroll
like the bundle of clothes
when a woman first surrenders herself
they burn
they melt
my soul is lit…
it evaporates steaming.
Send a rain to give it back to me!

They ostracised the wise old men
like insects
you are too disgusted to kill
but fear it will pollute your residence…
They walked for eons…
Feet bled upon the shards of ignorance
eyes emptied upon the wells of silence
mouths sealed with the certainty of absence.
They arrived at the dawn of time
found a breath of thyme
a gulp of cardamom
a bite of cinnamon.
Bound them into a cross

three tons upon their shoulders they now carry…

Look
they turned into sand grains
their fury avenges them!
Steel nails scratch the city's walls
blood waters the bulwarks
jaws creek
threads are cut
white eyes hammer the mind
reading anything we never dared confess
even to us…
and use it to strike!

Whispers creep down the chimneys
they silently circle their prey
the feeling of being watched
a sudden rustle behind you
light flickers
candles die down.
They say
evil has a way into your soul through the eyes
which is why darkness paralyzes me.
But…
Does everyone know?

One dead
ten dead
a million dead.

Rotten pieces
unrecognisable shards
of unidentifiable species
everywhere you dare rest your gaze upon
tombs.
Dreams, souls, loves, truths…
Their corpses
– or what you may craft as them.
And not even one person alive!
Are we alone on the planet, then?

Mirror games

I stand before the entrance
shaking
refusing to proceed
my stomach rebels
fighting
infuriated
opposing what I am about to do.
The door knob hot to the touch
the darkness crystalizes
steamy breaths escape my insides.
The door gives in with a loud creek
birds are startled by the sound explosion
they open their nightly wings
like scythes above the lethargical city
and take flight on the black canvas.

A scream
an empty corridor.
In 'Information'
a head is suspended mid-air
the neck almost detached
eternally pulled towards nothing
looks like a choked man once the hangman
opens the trapdoor
yet you can almost hear the perpetuating second

before the 'crack' of the bone.

His glance desperate
someone stole his noose
and he lost the meaning of hanging!
His body is missing
his point is missing
he cannot leave
he cannot remain suspended
his punishment
forever not knowing what he can do!

Cheap lights flicker
every now and then
the electric tzzzzt of a bulb erupts
like a slap
like a whip on those that climbed Calvary
while already being crucified.
A wheelchair
rusty
brown
strolls about the hallways
in and out of rooms it seems to go
as if looking for something
squeaking
making grieving sounds
mourning
slow
empty

in pain
as the lives of those haunting it.

A figure walks in the distance
white night gown
sad dirty slippers
predictable
resembling a prisoner's iron ball and chain.
She drags her feet
her path seems predetermined.
If I hold my breath long enough
just before my lungs saw my diaphragm for air
I see Time slowly cutting pieces off her
his jaws of white marble
gluttonously crunching her fragments
swallowing all that is perceived as being
leaving an empty carcass behind
barely moving
like a train
programmed to arrive a quarter to 3 outside the
hospital urinals.
The blood serum hangs from her arm
also dragging
following its mistress' routines.
She carries it
step by step
stinging
like her sins.

Sounds of children's toys
macabre and sickly-sweet little music.
Twirling eye-less ballerinas
arm-less gutted teddy bears
burnt dollies.
Kids laughing
soundless
without logical sequence
just laughing while holding a toy.
Where their eyes used to be
now gaping black holes scream in agony.
I do not approach
afraid
they might have the power to suck me in…

In my room there is a mirror
I see another room in its refection
with more ways out
scattered exits
ample choices
a variety of corners
open windows.
Anon, it confuses me…
I fail to understand
if the reflection is my real room
and the one I stand in the reflection's dream
or if my room wishes to be like its reflection
and is fighting for it…

Chess game

The room cavernous
cold stone sizzles upon its contact with the
flickering candle
the flame tongues lick the textured surface
like lovers of old
tedious in their exchanges
demanding in the eternal give and take
between their drawn swords
love is a battlefield.

In the centre of the four uneven walls stands a
table
its wood ancient
darkened by smoke arising from the fireplace
mould creeps up its pillars
like an unwanted touch
in a formal dinner
unseen
slithering upwards
always upwards.
Upon its surface
a chess
chiselled out of gutted granite
its pieces black and white .

They play
eons now they play
their game takes flesh
drawing sustenance from their own lives
nothing exists apart this room
this game
each ones slowly moves a limb
picks up a piece as cannon fodder
and proceeds
before letting their limb follow gravity once
more
ceasing to exist until their next turn.
Time has no meaning here
there are no clocks
no sand timers
nothing is alive aside the pieces on the board
and their breaths
cloudy stains upon the deadly still air that fills
the locked chamber.

Two players
one victor
tens of lives bleeding on the cursed granite
smashed
to please the opponent
sacrificed for a moment of glee
a faint smile upon lifeless
colourless lips
blue

as if kissed by cyanide.
The stench of Charon touches everything outside
the table
for he is waiting
patiently
to escort the loser onto his boat
passing the Acheron river
down into the pits of Hades.

He has several pieces protecting his King
a safe strategy
a build-up of experience and arrogance
infertile are her efforts
childish
he licks his canines in anticipation
a shiver runs through his muscles
she has the Queen and a horse
faint sweat paints her skin in glimmering
cascades of agony
Charon leans over from his iron chair
soon, he ponders.

He has her cornered.
Sure of his supremacy
he leans back
the leather chair squeaks
a sigh escapes his lips
like the soul of the recently departed
as it tries yet fails to ascend

the only way is down…
If only he knew…
She raises a pale hand
manicured nails
red as dragon's eyes catch the candle light
as she picks up the horse
one more futile loss – he easily triumphs against
it
a sardonic smirk appears on his aged face
the horse falls screaming its pain into the chasm
between them
as he makes his move and waits
waits for her fall
almost hungers for it
a show of obedience
a bowed existence in his service
oh how he yearns it...

Again
the manicured hand dances above the granite
her Queen locks eyes with her
both heads held high
feeling the wind weave their locks into ropes
both jaws clenched
too long
not allowing screams to escape
both hearts determined
one heart
she makes her move

the earth trembles with a terrorising guttural
sound
dust descends from the ceiling in response to the
shock
silence welcomes the new victor
Charon grasps his scythe as he stands up
her voice resonates upon the stone
sensual
loud
free
love is a battlefield
the only way is down
'Checkmate'.

Upon every dawn

Explosion
the earth is raised
caressing the sky.
Fire
another explosion.
Greatcoat
guns
combat boots
darkness
and EXPLOSION.
We run
taking cover behind the trenches
bodies pile up
arms
legs
heads
at times they may be attached
yet rarely…
Pieces scattered
mosaic tiles of flesh images
and all young!
Blood covers it all
like grandma's cosy blanket
weaved with love.

Above it all
sadness does not stem from the bodies
it comes from dreams
wave after wave
barely allowing a shaking breath between their
pauses.
Thousands of them
fragments
heart-crushing pieces of dreams
thrown without care everywhere
mute
burnt remnants
of lives unborn
limbo-residing…

Yet
your audacity wonders
why I do not allow myself some shuteye
as soon as the siren ceases its relentless wailing
and the ground stops
its nauseating dance?
Because I cannot…

Every night
I give birth to a child
flesh of our flesh
I ache for it
I bathe it
I dress it

I sing lullabies to it with a cracked voice
and every morning
they take it from me…
Just before dawn arrives
I hear them
my nose recognises their stench as they
approach
born out of destruction
each step of theirs on blades
and tightly grasping death.

They are four
I have never gazed upon their faces
their hands haunt me
rotten metal with glass nails
they snatch it from me!
They drag it behind them
like a sack, from its leg
like a petite bundle of despair
they drag it kilometres over ruins
and upon every dawn
they hang it…

Lethargy

Dragon's breath
a cloud outside the tower's window hides the
light
hides all else…
How was I found built in here?
Not a crack
not even a small hole aside this barred window.
What day is it?
What planet resides, I wonder, out there?
Was I … asleep?
Angry lethargy everywhere!
Green
obscene
night-rooted dragon's breath blurs everything
in
out
around me
lays upon the furniture
leaves blood-stained traces
alive tracks
scarlet fingerprints crawl on the wooden slabs
like sleepy snakes.
Please do not let it touch me anymore!

Bang!

Jaws
red jaws
decayed
sawed-off teeth
crunching
dismembering
making into pulp
their sound makes my gums sting in fear.
'Eat me'…
Behind the picture
behind the grey
owed
indebted and crippled years
it reads 'eat me'…
'Swallow me'…
On the hook that keeps it still
perpetuating
unchanging from time's slaughtering passage
still standing on the wall
it says 'swallow me'…

A black-and-white photo with the sea
a boat
a child
and a debt
open
like a wound that met gangrene…
I cannot eat anymore!
No more stuffing fits inside me!

Get me out!

Unclothe me from my shroud
make the sun pay his respects at my presence
with hammer and chisel
break my chains
no more gauze up my nostrils
trash the canopic jars
return everything back to me…
PUT THEM BACK!
I am still here!
Still drawing breath!
Forget me not!
My gods..
how many years…
How many lives was I asleep, mother?

Night's promise

Night came
as a dear friend
a trusty companion.
Ice-breathed
rain-scented
ash ink- painted in her glory
cloud-scattered and chill-invoking
darkly luminous
diamond-studded
bearing gifts of owls and sleepy mice
sheltering bats
kissing night flowers into bloom.

Night arrived
as a promised carriage
for a yearned voyage
a wanted trip
planned since the dawn of emotion.
Whispering of sweetness
desire
eyes gleaming like flickering fire
lips softer than the linens they lay upon
surrender
sighs and promises
in languages forgotten
intoxicating rush of red rivers

magic.

Night descended
like a verdict.
Lung-constricting gasps
claw-marked skin
soul-ripping echoes of screams
guilt
like a choke collar
around the trachea
shedding flayed skin with every move
every agonising breath
heavy
terror-inducing steps upon cobblestone
humanity a trinket
in a treasure chest
forever buried
voices
voices
voices.
And his name
upon their lipless mouths
a true and poisonous repetition
a venomous hiss
an arrow
dipped in aconite
that found its mark
buried deep within her chest
like an exclamation mark.

Beware of the horses

55

Shhh…
Sit down…
They will not enter our city tonight
everybody is gone
there is no one they will look for
no prey
nothing to take
it's just you and me my love.
Lay your weary head on my chest
and sleep
the pain will ease up in a while
and the spasms will stop
you shouldn't have gone out again
we could dine on patience
on silence once more…

Shhh…
Relax…
Those white things you saw outside the city
walls
were not tents
those were a herd of wild horses
tearing up the earth's surface with white flesh
those orange spots you noticed
were not thriving fires

they were their eyes
their fiery eyes
like fury inside a brazier
no
those sounds you heard
were not weapons clashing
it was thunder
under their hooves
as they were nailed in the soil
much like a newborn baby
latches on its mother's uterus to reach the light
those were not flags flapping
they were their manes and tails
like screams upon a blue backdrop
like the scalding moment just before murder
the shiny thing you saw was not iron
it was their muscles
like a pulsing river
amidst the sky
with a full moon.

Shhh…
Calm down…
Your temperature is not up
and the blood stopped blooming new roses on
the sheets
you will be fine come morning
no
those are not voices you hear

they are sounds made from the flowers
as they bleed the earth
pushing to make way for Spring
those are not footsteps outside the house
it's my heart
whispering to you
you re so close to her now
you learned to speak her language
no my love
no one broke down our door
a branch must have hit a shutter pushed from the
wind
much like a dead man's hand hits his coffin
at the moment of his resurrection
there's no one in the next room
those are not shadows of men you see
it's the fire
dancing on the walls
like a woman
seducing her mate
for the last time
that time that she surrenders her soul to him
bound in a kiss
before letting him walk onto death
without a shield
Do you love me?
Kiss me…!

All Rainbows are red!

Dawn shines red upon the city
yesterday's news swim
mutilated fragments in your mind
inside your bloodstream
sun's yellow meets your forehead
and shatters
into glass shards
lost
abducted by wind that gushes through.
Where have you gone?

You walk
pushing the breeze
pushing against incoming traffic
the road is grey
grey, not black
black is destined to be carried
on your shoulders.
All the cars are red…

Your memory now renovated
painted purple
huge flowers frame her rotten canvas
clouds descend upon your hands
leaving scorching marks

water leisurely drips onto the asphalt
it evaporates.
Purple is born when blue and red fuck.

Screams
someone is sobbing
indifference
life has chosen division
she cut herself into pieces
they hum like rivers as they carry people
none of them lead to the sea
crazed nerves hammer the brain
the arteries suffocate.
Arteries that are red.

Noon dominates the buildings
light whips concrete
mundane sounds circle the thoughts
experienced doctors used oscilloscopes on joy
now baffled at the flat line
no spikes
no twitches
of course, an alarm was raised.
A red alarm.
Where have you gone?

Boundaries break
double safety keys shatter
beyond need

above ability
tears rush into the avenues
drowning the roads
the riot is in full swing.
Waving red flags.

Mute footsteps
life flirting chimaeras
soundtrack of the hammer hitting the anvil
fire in the cellular level
smoke
brazier
lighting gas.
Sparks caressing red.

Blurred senses
permeating slivers
unable to unite
comatose recovery
particled advice
this year
we decorated the Christmas tree out in the street
filled with blue balls
little silver glass pieces
and red lights.

Friends' cocktail swims green in your cup in the
afternoon

dark coffee
music
a deep inhale of cancer
something fell on the marble floor dead
something twitches outside in the cold
you kick them both
out of your way.
The voice on the cd player is red.
Where have you gone?

Flesh burns under the shower water
past flakes away
drowns itself in the drain
small droplets paused upon your shoulders and
breasts
warm towel
pain
ignorance shoves her nails on the mirror
your gaze is filled with scars.
Red wounds cover your body.

Off-white silence shatters your eardrums
eyes rest upon wooden brown doors
closed doors
night is coming
numb perception
hollow subconscious
good evening, lady Sorrow.
The sky is flaming red.

Black graffiti on the stones
walls shout their anger at passers by
posters along the highways
pink posters
little promises
biting betrayals
pupil follows bitterness
they both dilate the same
footsteps become thuds.
Pink comes in through the door the white opens
to come into red.

Evening
swirling of a sea you named once
something is missing from the concrete monster
an instruction manual!
Sharp traps
laid out like a carpet come winter
no, not the easy way out
who swallowed the light?
Sharp pain
soul splits apart
finally revealing the eggs inside.
Blood runs red.

Pride is torn
a spear whistles as it flies
tigress' eyes scan the air

silent desperation
abrupt violence
anger
adrenaline
the body starts to shake
the volcano is about to erupt
burning
cosmo-altering lava.
Adrenaline hits red.

Muffled path
map is torn
X does not mark the spot
X marks nothing
death rattles
last feast before the final departure
chest feels a ton
a hand is raised
only to fall back down again
siren sounds
lights keep flashing.
Blue-Red-Blue-Red.

Cold creeps in
to embrace that which no one else accepts
the outcast
the forgotten
the broken and bruised
the stitched up puzzle

with too many pieces missing
the sky crashes upon the lonely figure with great
speed
marks upon the shoulders
from lifting stones
old, white marks
deep memories with every textured slice of flesh
put another green thorn on the score
we won again tonight
the night is smashed into a million yells
in the corner.
Your eyes red.
Where are you going…?